Ladders

Rain and Shine

TWO CAN

Published by
Two-Can Publishing
A division of Zenith Entertainment plc
43-45 Dorset Street
London W1H 4AB

Created by
act-two
346 Old Street
London EC1V 9RB

Written by: Deborah Kespert
Story by: Sue Barraclough
Editor: Sarah Levete
Consultant: Barbara Taylor
Main illustrations: Fran Jordan
Computer illustrations: James Evans
Cover illustration: Steve Holmes
Designer: Lisa Nutt
Art director: Belinda Webster
Pre-press production manager: Adam Wilde
Picture researcher: Jenny West

Hardback ISBN 1-85434-653-9
Paperback ISBN 1-85434-866-3

Dewey Decimal Classification 551.5

Hardback 10 9 8 7 6 5 4 3 2 1
Paperback 10 9 8 7 6 5 4 3 2 1

A catalogue record for this book is available from the British Library.

Photographic credits: p4: Image Bank; p5: Tony Stone Images; p6: Tony Stone Images;
p7: Telegraph Colour Library; p8: Tony Stone Images; p11: Tony Stone Images;
p15: Still Pictures; p16: Two-Can Design; p17: Telegraph Colour Library; p18: Pictures Colour Library;
p19: Retna; p20: Collections/Anthea Sieveking; p22 Tony Stone Images; p23: Bruce Coleman Ltd.

Printed in Hong Kong by Wing King Tong

What's inside?

This book tells you about different types of weather. You can find out how the weather changes during the year and what happens to plants and animals through the seasons.

 # Clouds and rain

Look up at the sky! Can you see any clouds? Are they white and fluffy or dark and gloomy? Clouds are made up of tiny drops of water. The drops grow bigger and heavier until they fall to the ground. It's raining!

This grey **cloud** is full of water and has just burst open!

Splish, splosh! Lots of **raindrops** patter on your hat.

When it pours with rain, **puddles** of water are left on the ground.

Fog is a type of cloud that touches the ground. On a foggy day, it's hard to see in front of you.

A **raincoat** keeps out the water. Inside, you stay cosy and dry.

This beautiful band of colours is called a rainbow. It appears when there is rain and sunshine at the same time.

This dog has dripping **wet** fur, so it shakes itself dry. Watch out for the splashes!

Can you see the wavy **ripples** in the water?

 Wind

You can't see the wind, but you can feel it on your skin. Sometimes, the wind feels warm, but at other times it's icy cold. These pictures show you what can happen on windy days.

A **gentle breeze** makes your socks and T-shirts flap about on the washing line.

The wind is blowing hard enough to push this windsurfer across the choppy blue sea.

Whoosh! In a **strong breeze**, these colourful kites soar high into the air.

Look out! A sudden **gust** of wind can turn your umbrella inside out!

In a strong **gale**, the wind whistles through the trees. Leaves fly everywhere.

In a few parts of the world, a fierce wind, called a tornado, whizzes round like a spinning top.

It's a fact!

A fierce tornado can be so powerful that it can lift a long, mighty train high up into the air!

 # It's a storm!

When clouds in the sky loom big and dark, and the wind starts to howl, you know a storm is on the way. Suddenly, rain pours down. A storm can be exciting, but make sure you stay safely inside your home.

It's raining so hard that the road has started to **flood**.

Dazzling lightning is a giant spark of electricity from a thundercloud. It lights up the sky for a few seconds.

A huge grey **thundercloud** covers the sky.

eavy rain is called
downpour. It makes
drumming noise
the roof.

It's a fact!

During a storm, lumps of ice, called hailstones, may fall from the sky. The largest hailstones ever spotted were as big a tennis balls!

A flash of bright white **lightning** streaks through the murky sky.

Boom! Can you hear the loud **thunderclap**?

❄ Snow and ice

On an extremely cold day, snow falls from the sky and covers the ground like a white carpet. You can make funny shapes out of soft, fresh snow. If it's freezing cold, the snow turns into hard, slippery ice.

Water in the clouds freezes into white **snowflakes**, which fall gently to the ground.

It's a fact!

In some of the coldest parts of the world, people build shelters, called igloos, out of snow and slabs of ice.

A smiling **snowman** lasts for as long as the weather stays icy cold.

The wind blows the snow into a big pile, called a **snowdrift**.

Long, sharp **icicles** are frozen drips of water.

It's fun to make **footprints** in the crunchy snow!

Look at this delicate, lacy snowflake. Each tiny flake of snow has a different pattern.

Our family snaps

Take a look at the
holiday photographs in
our album. Holidays are
fun come rain or shine!

What do you think the children are making in the snow?

Words you know

Here are some words that you learned earlier. Say them out loud, then try to find the things in the picture.

snowflakes   raincoat
rainbow   puddle
storm   kite

What helps to keep the girl dry in the rain?

What happens when it's sunny and rainy at the same time?

Changing Seasons

Our year has four seasons, called spring, summer, autumn and winter. Each season brings its own kind of weather. As the weather warms up and cools down, look out for all kinds of changes that happen.

spring

In spring, there are lots of **rain showers**. The sun begins to shine more warmly, too.

It's a fact!

When it's winter and chilly in the top half of the world, it's summer and sunny in the bottom half of the world!

winter

In winter, it may start to **snow**. This is the coldest time of year.

In summer, the **sun** is high
in the sky and shines brightly.
This is the hottest time of year.

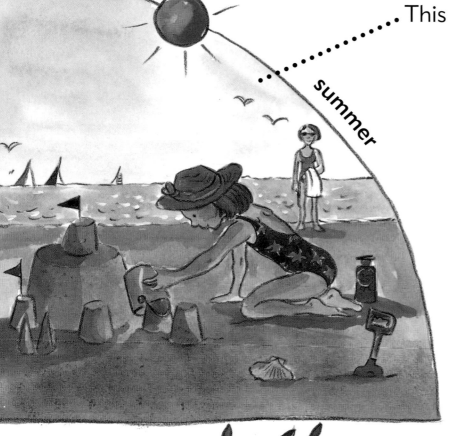

summer

Some countries have only two seasons,
one dry and one rainy. In the rainy
season, it can pour down for months!

In autumn, strong
winds blow and the
days turn cooler.

autumn

Warm Spring

In spring, the weather warms up and the days become longer. Now that the cold winter is over, plants push out of the ground and new leaves start to grow. Lots of baby animals are born, too.

New **leaves** on the trees are bright green.

Hundreds of tiny **buds** start to unfold.

Gardeners are busy at this time of year. Gentle rain and warm sunshine help young plants to grow quickly.

Spring is a colourful season. The first **flowers** start to bloom.

A baby **lamb** has a thick woollen coat to keep it warm on cooler days.

A bird has built a snug **nest** out of twigs and leaves.

The bird lays **eggs** in the nest. The eggs will hatch late in the spring.

These fluffy ducklings are a few weeks old. There is plenty of food to eat, so soon they will be big and strong.

 Hot summer

In summer, the days are long and warm. You can play outside when the sun shines brightly and the sky is blue. Insects buzz and flutter around gardens, which are packed with colourful, scented flowers.

The warm golden **sunshine** helps the flowers to bloom.

A stripy bumblebee lands on a flower. The bee collects a sweet juice, called nectar, to make into honey.

It's fun to splash around in the **water**.

A **sun hat** helps keep you cool on a hot summer day.

Never look directly at the sun. It could damage your eyes.

Make sure you rub plenty of sunblock into your skin. It will help to protect your skin from the strong sunshine.

The cat looks comfortable, lazing in the cool **shade**.

Bright **butterflies** flutter through the garden.

Cool autumn

On an autumn day, it's fresh and cool, even when the sun shines. Early in the morning, the air may feel damp. Trees lose their leaves, fruit ripens and animals prepare for the cold winter months ahead.

Before leaves fall from **branches**, they turn rusty red and gold.

Gusts of wind make the autumn leaves **blow** everywhere!

Juicy red apples are ready to be picked from the tree. This apple tastes sweet!

A **squirrel** collects nuts, which it stores, then eats during the cold winter.

There are tasty **nuts** for animals to eat.

These **birds** are about to fly to a warmer place far away. They'll return in the spring.

It's a fact!

A squirrel hides nuts for the winter in all kinds of nooks and crannies, but sometimes it forgets where it has put them!

Chilly winter

In winter, days are short and nights are long. The sun shines weakly and the weather turns cold. Many animals hide away until the warm spring, but others are up and about during the chilly weather.

Many trees lose their leaves. Some of them are completely **bare**.

It's so cold that the water in this pond has frozen into **ice**.

This plant is covered in a coat of frost. It looks like icing on a cake!

Even in freezing winter, **fir trees** keep their leaves, called needles.

Whoops! This duck is **skating** on the slippery ice.

There's little food for birds to eat, except winter **berries**.

In the cold winter months, a dormouse sleeps in a cosy nest. It won't wake up until the warm spring arrives.

Seasons collage

Look at this colourful collage of things to make. It's the perfect way to keep a record of changes through the seasons.

24

autumn

winter

Words you know

Here are some words that you learned earlier. Say them out loud, then try to find the things in the picture.

leaves   **butterflies**
squirrel   **berries**
lambs   **flowers**

How many fluttering butterflies can you count?

Grandma's amazing weather machine

WHAM, BANG, CRASH! As usual, mysterious noises were coming from Grandma's workshop...

Daisy just loved staying with her grandparents. She was especially excited because Grandpa had promised to take her to the safari park on Saturday. Daisy couldn't wait to see the latest arrival, which was a fierce tiger!

The only thing that bothered Daisy was Grandma's silly inventions. Today, Grandma was even busier than usual, tinkering around in her workshop.

"You'll never guess what I've invented this time, Daisy," said Grandma excitedly.

"I have no idea," smiled Daisy.

"It's an amazing weather forecasting machine that will always be right! I'm tired of the weather people being wrong all the time. I know I can do better!" explained Grandma.

She pulled out a spanner and tweaked a huge dial on the front of the machine.

"That should do it. Just wait and see," said Grandma.

OVERLOAD

OFF   ON

On Wednesday, Daisy came down for breakfast and bumped into Grandma coming out of her workshop.

"It's going to snow today," warned Grandma. "We'll have to wrap up warmly to go shopping." Daisy put on her coat, hat and scarf, and stepped outside into bright sunshine.

"Phew, it's hot! Are you sure it's going to snow, Grandma?" asked Daisy.

"Of course!" replied Grandma. "You'll be able to make a snowman after lunch."

As the morning wore on, Daisy grew hotter and hotter in her winter clothes.

"Hmmm," said Grandma thoughtfully. "My machine needs a little more work."

When they arrived home, Grandma disappeared into her workshop.

BANG! CRASH! SQUEAK! TWEAK!

"That should do it. My machine will get it right next time," promised Grandma.

Thursday morning was dark and grey, but Grandma was planning a picnic.

"Put your shorts on," she said confidently, "today, it will be warm and sunny."

"But Grandma," said Daisy, "look at those big thunderclouds."

"No buts, Daisy. My weather machine will be right." But by the time they reached the park, big fat raindrops fell steadily from the clouds.

Grandma handed out soggy sandwiches.

"I'm sure it will brighten up any minute," she said. Soon it was pouring with rain, so they all trudged home, dripping wet.

"Never mind, Daisy," said Grandpa. "We'll have a great time at the safari park on Saturday."

RUSTLE! RUMMAGE! SNAP! TAP!

"That should do it. My machine will get it right next time," said Grandma. That evening, Daisy found Grandma sorting out paint and paintbrushes.

"My weather machine says it will be calm and still tomorrow," announced Grandma. "Perfect weather to give the shed a lick of paint."

So on Friday morning, Daisy and Grandma put on their overalls and went outside. A strong breeze sent the clouds scudding across the sky. Sudden gusts of wind picked up dry leaves and sent them swirling around. The leaves collided with the shed and stuck to it, ruining Daisy and Grandma's careful work.

"It looks like the weather machine was wrong again!" moaned Daisy.

"Humph!" Grandma replied as she scurried back to her workshop.

SAW! GRIND! WHIRR! GRRRR!

"That should do it. My machine will get it right next time," said Grandma.

On Saturday morning, Daisy could hardly contain her excitement. Today she was going to the safari park to see a real-life tiger. Today would be great whatever the weather did!

But Grandma was in a flap.

"My weather machine says a giant tornado is heading our way! I must warn everyone," she cried.

Daisy couldn't believe her ears.

"But the sun's shining," Daisy argued, "and Grandpa's taking me to the safari park!"

"There's no way you can go outside. It's far too dangerous," Grandma said firmly.

Grandma knocked on every door in the street, telling everyone to stay inside with the doors and windows closed. Then she phoned her friends and relatives.

Suddenly a newsflash appeared on the television:

VERY URGENT WARNING! DANGEROUS TIGER ON THE LOOSE! STAY INSIDE WITH YOUR DOORS AND WINDOWS SHUT!

The message spread in minutes. Soon the whole town was deserted. No children played in the gardens, no neighbours chatted over the fence, no postmen strolled down the street. There was complete silence as everyone waited for the terrible tornado to arrive.

Daisy, Grandma and Grandpa couldn't believe it. A mighty tiger was wandering down the empty street.

"Wow!" whispered Daisy. "A real-life tiger right outside the house! We didn't even have to go to the safari park to see it!"

The whole town watched open-mouthed as the park rangers arrived. They lured the tiger safely into a cage, then drove it back to the safari park.

People poured out of their houses, laughing and chatting. A crowd gathered outside Grandma's house and cheered as she opened her front door.

"How on earth did everyone manage to get indoors so quickly?" asked a reporter from the local paper.

"It was Daisy's grandma," said a boy. "She warned us about a t-t-t…"

"Tiger!" said Daisy quickly.

"Incredible!" said the reporter, scribbling in his notebook. "So Daisy's grandma saved the day!"

"Yes," laughed Daisy proudly, "she certainly did!"

Puzzles

Double trouble!

Look at these two pictures of a rainy day. Can you spot four differences between picture a and picture b?

Close up!

We've zoomed in on different kinds of weather. Can you guess what's going on in each picture?

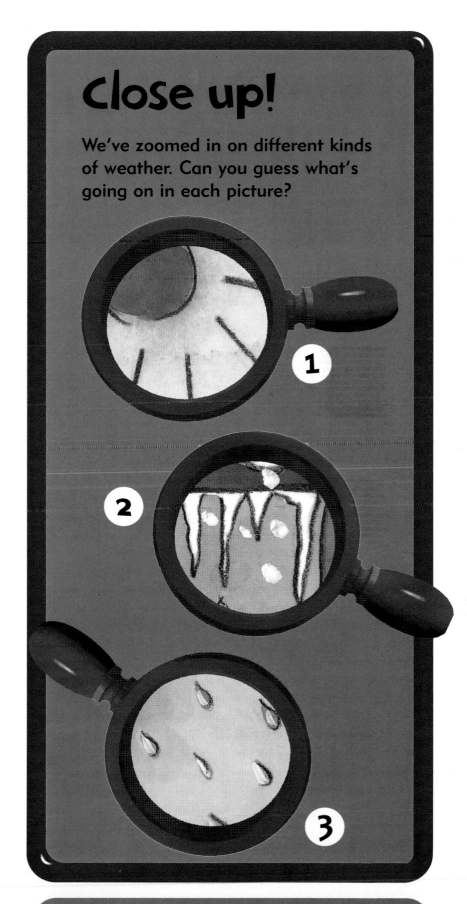

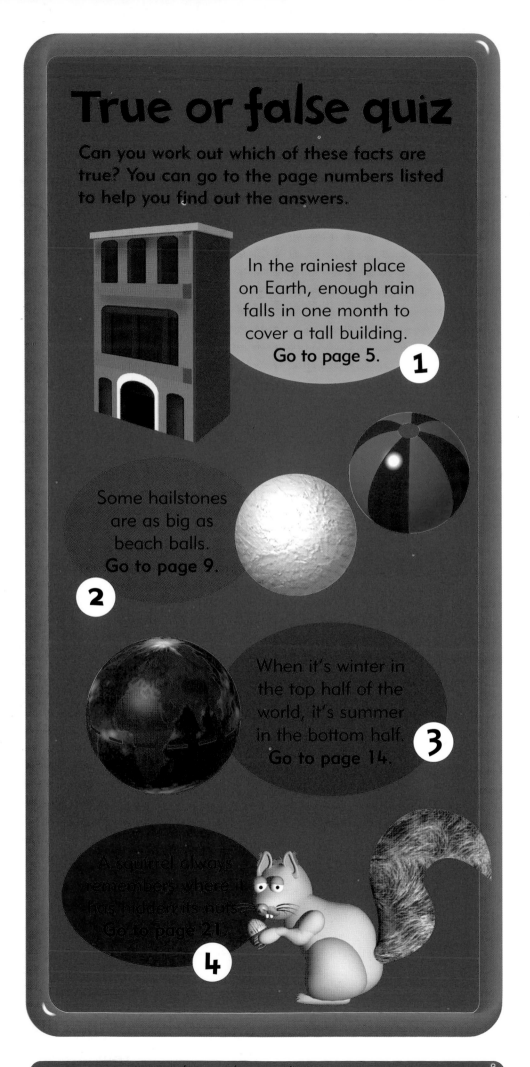

True or false quiz

Can you work out which of these facts are true? You can go to the page numbers listed to help you find out the answers.

In the rainiest place on Earth, enough rain falls in one month to cover a tall building.
Go to page 5.
1

Some hailstones are as big as beach balls.
Go to page 9.
2

When it's winter in the top half of the world, it's summer in the bottom half.
Go to page 14.
3

A squirrel always remembers where it has hidden its nuts.
Go to page 21.
4

Index